BIG 'n Easy Mini Quilts

by Christiane Meunier

CHITRA PUBLICATIONS

Your Best Value in Quilting

Chitra Publications
2 Public Avenue
Montrose, Pennsylvania 18801-1220

First Printing: 1998

Library of Congress Cataloging-in-Publication Data

Meunier, Christiane, 1952-
    Big 'n easy mini quilts / by Christiane Meunier.
        p.   cm.
    ISBN 1-885588-18-6
    1. Quilting--Patterns. 2. Patchwork--Patterns. 3. Miniature
quilts. I. Title.
    TT835.M485   1998
    746.46'041--dc21

97-48883
CIP

Edited by: Deborah Hearn and Debra Feece
Design and Illustrations: Diane M. Albeck-Grick
Cover Photography: Guy Cali Associates, Inc., Clarks Summit, Pennsylvania
Inside Photography: Guy Cali Associates, Inc., Clarks Summit, Pennsylvania;
Van Zandbergen Photography, Brackney, Pennsylvania;
Stephen J. Appel Photography, Vestal, New York.

Our Mission Statement:

*We publish quality quilting magazines and books
that recognize, promote and inspire self-expression.
We are dedicated to serving our customers
with respect, kindness and efficiency.*

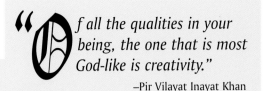

"Of all the qualities in your being, the one that is most God-like is creativity."

–Pir Vilayat Inayat Khan

Introduction

Welcome to *Big 'n Easy Mini Quilts*. As the publisher of *Miniature Quilts* magazine, I spend much of my time talking to quilters and thinking about what it is that they look for in a quilt pattern. I wanted this, my first book, to give quilters what they desire most—beautiful quilts that can be made quickly.

Beyond that, I wanted to take the opportunity to invite quilters into my home. This book has allowed me to do that for the quilts were photographed there.

I enjoyed decorating my home with the 17 irresistible little quilts that you'll find patterned here. While I was arranging these delightful minis for the photo shoot, I thought about how much you'll enjoy displaying them in your home as well, or giving them to special friends.

These are quilts that were fun to select or design and quick-as-a-wink to make. In fact, you'll find easy quick-cutting and piecing directions that make it possible to sew most of them in a single evening! And, knowing that many quilters shy away from making quilts with tiny pieces, I've included special construction techniques so you'll never have to handle a piece of fabric smaller than 1"!

Believing that "variety is the spice of life," quilts have been included for all tastes. Whether you like classic traditional quilts, charming country quilts or quilts that are purely fun and fanciful, you'll find patterns that you'll want to make in *Big 'n Easy Mini Quilts*. So, whether you're an experienced quilter or a beginner, turn the page and get in on the fun. This book was written for you, and an enchanting little quilt is just an evening away.

Christiane

I'd like to thank "the sacred circle" for the impetus that got me started on this book and encouragement along the way. Thanks also to every member of the Chitra Publications family for the professional and emotional support they provided and to Joanie Keith for the unique and masterful quilting she added to several of my quilts.

Table of Contents

Blues Bayou

Have fun with your
fabric stash!

"Blues Bayou" (21" square) was stitched by Carol J. Lewis of Fresno, California. Carol used a variation of the Flock of Geese block and her scrap bag of blues to create a quilt that really sparkles. It is reminiscent of light reflecting off the ripples of water in a pool.

QUILT SIZE: 21" square
BLOCK SIZE: 4" square

MATERIALS
Yardage is estimated for 44" fabric.
- Assorted scraps of blue prints totaling 3/8 yard
- 1/4 yard light print
- 5" x 18" strip of green
- 1/3 yard blue print
- 23" square of backing fabric
- 23" square of thin batting

CUTTING
Dimensions include a 1/4" seam allowance.
- Cut 64: 1 7/8" squares, blue prints
- Cut 16: 2 7/8" squares, blue prints
- Cut 64: 1 7/8" squares, light print
- Cut 16: 2 7/8" squares, light print
- Cut 2: 1" x 16 1/2" strips, green, for the inner border
- Cut 2: 1" x 17 1/2" strips, green, for the inner border
- Cut 2: 2 1/4" x 17 1/2" strips, blue print, for the outer border
- Cut 2: 2 1/4" x 21" strips, blue print, for the outer border
- Cut 4: 1 3/4" x 30" strips, blue print, for the binding

DIRECTIONS
- Draw a diagonal line from corner to corner on the wrong side of each 1 7/8" light print square.
- Lay a 1 7/8" light print square on a 1 7/8" blue print square, right sides together. Stitch 1/4" away from the line on both sides. Make 64.

- Cut each square on the drawn line. You will have 128 small pieced squares. Press the seam allowances toward the blue print.
- Lay out 4 pieced squares in 2 rows of 2. Stitch the squares into rows and join the rows to create a Four Square, as shown. Make 32. Set them aside.

- Draw a diagonal line from corner to corner on the wrong side of each 2 7/8" light print square. Lay a 2 7/8" light print square on a 2 7/8" blue print square and stitch 1/4" away from the line on both sides. Make 16.
- Cut each square on the drawn line. You will have 32 large pieced squares.
- Lay out 2 large pieced squares and 2 Four Squares. Stitch the squares into rows and join the rows to complete a block, as shown. Make 16.

- Lay out the blocks in 4 rows of 4, as shown.

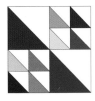

- Stitch the blocks into rows and join the rows.

- Stitch the 1" x 16 1/2" green strips to opposite sides of the quilt.
- Stitch the 1" x 17 1/2" green strips to the remaining sides of the quilt.
- Stitch the 2 1/4" x 17 1/2" blue print strips to opposite sides of the quilt.
- Stitch the 2 1/4" x 21" blue print strips to the remaining sides of the quilt.
- Finish according to *Stitching Tips*, using the 1 3/4" blue print strips for the binding. — BIG Easy

Shoo Fly

Cute, colorful and quick to stitch!

Here's an old-time favorite to stitch in bright colors! I used 5 dominant colors in my mini and added one bright green square as a surprise. **"Shoo Fly"** (17 1/2" x 23 1/8") is my scaled-down version of Polly Briwa's full-size "Churn Dash" quilt which was published in Issue 46 of *Quilting Today* magazine

QUILT SIZE: 17 1/2" x 23 1/8"
BLOCK SIZE: 3" square

MATERIALS
Yardage is estimated for 44" fabric.
• Fat eighth (11" x 18") each of 5 different color prints (I used gold, red, purple, dark gray and navy blue)
• 1/4 yard muslin print
• Scrap of green print at least 1 1/2" square
• 1/4 yard fabric of your choice for the binding
• 19 1/2" x 25 1/2" piece of backing fabric
• 19 1/2" x 25 1/2" piece of thin batting

CUTTING
Dimensions include a 1/4" seam allowance.
From each of 5 color prints:
• Cut 2: 3 3/4" squares
• Cut 2: 1 1/2" x 7" strips
• Cut 14: 1 1/2" squares
From the muslin print:
• Cut 48: 1 1/2" x 3 1/2" strips, for the sashing
• Cut 20: 1 1/2" squares
• Cut 10: 3 3/4" squares
• Cut 5: 1 1/2" x 7" strips

Also:
• Cut 1: 1 1/2" square, green print
• Cut 1: 5 1/2" square from 3 of the color prints; then cut it in quarters diagonally to yield 12 setting triangles. You will use 10. NOTE: *If you wish to have more colors represented in the setting triangles, cut 5 1/2" squares from additional prints.*
• Cut 2: 3" squares from each of 2 fabrics, then cut each in half diagonally to yield 4 corner triangles
• Cut 3: 1 3/4" x 44" strips, binding fabric

DIRECTIONS
• Draw diagonal lines from corner to corner on the wrong side of a 3 3/4" muslin print square. Draw a horizontal and a vertical line through the center. Make 10.

• Lay a 3 3/4" muslin print square on a color print 3 3/4" square, right sides

together. Stitch 1/4" away from the diagonal lines on both sides, as shown. Make 10.

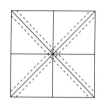

• Cut each square on the drawn diagonal, horizontal and vertical lines. Each sewn square yields 8 pieced squares for a total of 80. Press the seam allowances toward the color print. Group the pieced squares by color.
• Stitch a 1 1/2" x 7" muslin print strip between 2 matching 1 1/2" x 7" color print strips to make a pieced strip. Make 5.
• Cut four 1 1/2" slices from each pieced strip to yield 20 center rows. Set them aside.

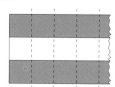

• Stitch a 1 1/2" color print square between 2 matching pieced squares to

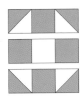

• Lay out a center row and 2 matching pieced rows.

• Join the rows to make a Shoo Fly block. Make 20. You will use 18.
• Referring to the Assembly Diagram as necessary, lay out 18 Shoo Fly blocks, on point. Place the 1 1/2" muslin print sashing strips between the blocks. Place the remaining 1 1/2" color print squares and the 1 1/2" green print square between the sashing strips. Place

the setting triangles in the spaces around the sides and a corner triangle in each corner.
• Stitch the sashing strips to the blocks to make diagonal rows. Stitch the appropriate setting and corner triangles to the ends of the rows.
• Join the 1 1/2" color print squares and sashing strips to make pieced sashing strips.
• Join the block rows and pieced sashing strips.
• Trim the ends of the pieced sashing strips even with the edge of the setting and corner triangles.
• Finish according to *Stitching Tips*, using the 1 3/4" strips for the binding.

Assembly Diagram

Liberty Star

Stitch this mini for yourself—
in red, white, and blue!

"Liberty Star" (20" x 26"), a primitive miniature with a country theme, was stitched by Sharon Meinz of Brooklyn Park, Minnesota. What a delightful way to display your patriotism! A quilted heart in the upper left-hand corner of each flag adds a charming detail.

QUILT SIZE: 20" x 26"
BLOCK SIZE: 6" square

MATERIALS
Yardage is estimated for 44" fabric.
• Assorted scraps of light, medium and dark prints in gold, blue, red and tan
• Fat quarter (18" x 22") tan
• Fat quarter red print
• 1/4 yard tan print for the binding

• 22" x 28" piece of backing fabric
• 22" x 28" piece of thin batting

CUTTING
Pattern pieces are full size and include a 1/4" seam allowance, as do all dimensions given. When using templates, R means to reverse the template before cutting.
NOTE: *Choose five fabrics for each block. You will use one print for the*

background and one for the star points. You will use 3 "flag prints"; one blue, one red and one light. Refer to the photo for help in choosing your fabrics.
For each of 6 blocks:
• Cut 4: 2" squares, background print
• Cut 4: A, background print
• Cut 4: B, star point print
• Cut 4: C, star point print

7

- Cut 1: 1 3/4" x 2" rectangle, blue "flag print"
- Cut 1: D, red "flag print"
- Cut 1: DR, red "flag print"
- Cut 1: F, red "flag print"
- Cut 1: E, light "flag print"
- Cut 1: F, light "flag print"

Also:
- Cut 2: 1 3/4" x 18 1/2" strips, tan, for the inner border
- Cut 2: 1 3/4" x 15" strips, tan, for the inner border
- Cut 2: 3" x 21" strips, red print, for the outer border
- Cut 2: 3" x 20" strips, red print, for the outer border
- Cut 3: 1 3/4" x 44" strips, tan print, for the binding

DIRECTIONS

- Stitch a background print A between a matching print B and C to make a pieced rectangle. Make 4.

- Stitch a pieced rectangle between two 2" background print squares to make a pieced strip. Make 2. Set them aside.

- Stitch the light "flag print" E between the matching red "flag print" D and DR to make Unit 1.
- Stitch Unit 1 to a 1 3/4" x 2" blue print rectangle to make the top flag section.

- Stitch the light "flag print" F and the red "flag print" F together to make Unit 2.

- Stitch Unit 2 to the top flag section to complete the flag.

- Stitch the flag between 2 pieced rectangles to make a flag unit.

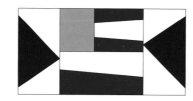

- Stitch the flag unit between 2 pieced strips, to complete the block. Make 6.

ASSEMBLY

- Lay out the blocks in 3 rows of 2, referring to the photo as needed.
- Stitch the blocks into rows and join the rows.
- Stitch the 1 3/4" x 18 1/2" tan strips to the long sides of the quilt.
- Stitch the 1 3/4" x 15" tan strips to the short sides of the quilt.
- Stitch the 3" x 21" red print strips to the long sides of the quilt.
- Stitch the 3" x 20" red print strips to the short sides of the quilt.
- Finish according to *Stitching Tips*, using the 1 3/4" tan print strips for the binding.
- Quilt as desired. —————— BIG Easy

Full-Size Quilting Design

Full-Size Patterns for Liberty Star

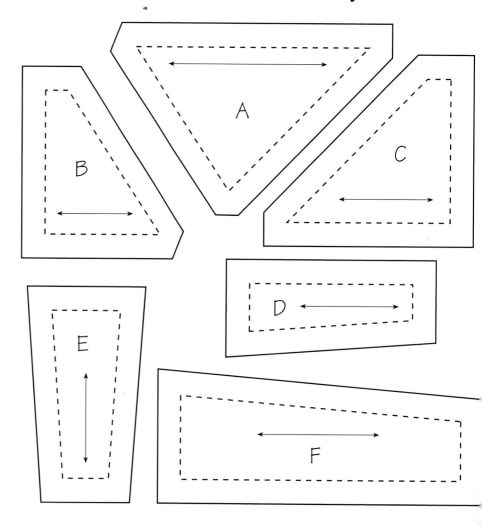

Square-in-a-Square

Set squares in motion with lots of light and dark fabrics!

How was the sense of movement in **"Square-in-a-Square"** (20" x 24") achieved? Alternating most of the central squares with light and dark fabrics makes the viewer's eye "hop" from one square to the next while the brown paisley triangles do their own "dance."

QUILT SIZE: 20" x 24"
BLOCK SIZE: 4" square

MATERIALS
Yardage is estimated for 44" fabric.
• Assorted scraps of light and dark prints
• 1/8 yard tan print
• 1/2 yard green print
• 22" x 26" piece of backing fabric
• 22" x 26" piece of thin batting

CUTTING
Dimensions include a 1/4" seam allowance.
• Cut 5: A, assorted light prints; or cut five 2 1/2" squares
• Cut 28: B, assorted light prints in matching sets of 4; or cut fourteen 2 3/8" squares in matching sets of 2, then cut each in half diagonally to yield 7 sets of 4 triangles
• Cut 28: C, assorted light prints in matching sets of 4; or cut fourteen 2 7/8" squares in matching sets of 2, then cut each in half diagonally to yield 7 sets of 4 triangles
• Cut 7: A, assorted dark prints; or cut seven 2 1/2" squares
• Cut 20: B, dark prints in matching sets of 4; or cut ten 2 3/8" squares in matching sets of 2, then cut each in half diagonally to yield 5 sets of 4 triangles
• Cut 20: C, assorted dark prints in matching sets of 4; or cut ten 2 7/8" squares in matching sets of 2, then cut each in half diagonally to yield 5 sets of 4 triangles
• Cut 2: 1 1/4" x 12 1/2" strips, green print, for the inner border
• Cut 2: 1 1/4" x 18" strips, green print, for the inner border
• Cut 2: 3/4" x 14" strips, tan print, for the middle border
• Cut 2: 3/4" x 18 1/2" strips, tan print, for the middle border
• Cut 2: 3 1/4" x 14 1/2" strips, green print, for the outer border
• Cut 2: 3 1/4" x 24" strips, green print, for the outer border
• Cut 3: 1 3/4" x 44" strips, green print, for the binding

DIRECTIONS
For each of 12 blocks:
Group an A, a set of 4 matching B's and a set of 4 matching C's. Notice the contrast in values between the fabrics within each block.
• Stitch 4 matching dark B's to the sides of a light print A to make a larger square.

• Stitch 4 matching light C's to the sides of the larger square, to complete a Square-in-a-Square block. Make 5.

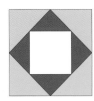

• In the same manner, stitch matching light B's to the sides of a dark A. Stitch matching dark C's to the unit to make a block. Make 7.

ASSEMBLY
• Lay out the blocks in 4 rows of 3, referring to the photo for placement.
• Stitch the blocks into rows. Join the rows.
• Stitch the 1 1/4" x 12 1/2" green print strips to the short sides of the quilt.
• Stitch the 1 1/4" x 18" green print strips to the remaining sides of the quilt.
• Stitch the 3/4" x 14" tan print ☞

strips to the short sides of the quilt.
• Stitch the 3/4" x 18 1/2" tan print strips to the remaining sides of the quilt.
• Stitch the 3 1/4" x 14 1/2" green print strips to the short sides of the quilt.
• Stitch the 3 1/4" x 24" green print strips to the remaining sides of the quilt.
• Finish according to *Stitching Tips*, using the 1 3/4" green print strips for the binding. ——— BIG°Easy

Full-Size Patterns for Square-in-a-Square

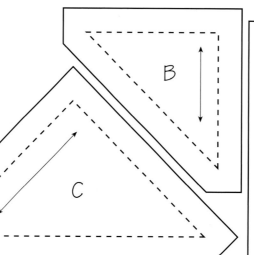

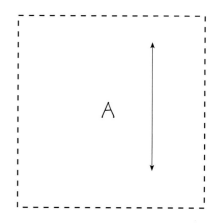

Spools

The perfect quilt for your favorite plaids and stripes!

Here's a decorative way to use some of your favorite plaids and stripes. Debra Feece of Montrose, Pennsylvania, stitched **"Spools"** (22 1/2" square) using bits and pieces from her scrap pile. You'll find that sewing goes quickly with the easy-to-handle pieces.

QUILT SIZE: 22 1/2" square
BLOCK SIZE: 3 1/2" square

MATERIALS
Yardage is estimated for 44" fabric.
• Assorted scraps of light, medium and dark plaids and stripes each at least 5 1/2" square
• Fat eighth (11" x 18") tan stripe
• 1/3 yard burgundy print
• 25" square of backing fabric
• 25" square of thin batting

CUTTING
Pattern pieces are full size and include a 1/4" seam allowance, as do all dimensions given.

For each of the 16 Spool blocks:
• Cut 1: A, plaid or stripe; or cut one 1 3/4" square
• Cut 2: B, same plaid or stripe
• Cut 2: B, contrasting plaid or stripe
Also:
• Cut 2: 1 1/4" x 14 1/2" strips, burgundy print, for the inner border
• Cut 2: 1 1/4" x 16" strips, burgundy print, for the inner border
• Cut 2: 1 1/2" x 16" strips, tan stripe, for the middle border
• Cut 2: 1 1/2" x 18" strips, tan stripe, for the middle border
• Cut 2: 2 3/4" x 18" strips, burgundy print, for the outer border
• Cut 2: 2 3/4" x 22 1/2" strips, bur-

gundy print, for the outer border
• Cut 3: 1 3/4" x 44" strips, burgundy print, for the binding

DIRECTIONS
For the Spool blocks:
• Take the pieces for one block and stitch two plaid or stripe B's to opposite sides of the matching A. Start and stop stitching 1/4" from the edges, as shown.

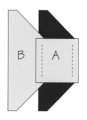

• Stitch the contrasting B's to the remaining sides of the A in the same manner.

• Join the B's at each corner to complete the Spool block. Make 16.

• Lay out the blocks in 4 rows of 4, alternating the direction of the spools.
• Stitch the blocks into rows. Join the rows.

• Stitch the 1 1/4" x 14 1/2" burgundy print strips, to opposite sides of the quilt.
• Stitch the 1 1/4" x 16" burgundy print strips, to the remaining sides of the quilt.
• Stitch the 1 1/2" x 16" tan stripe strips, to opposite sides of the quilt.
• Stitch the 1 1/2" x 18" tan stripe strips, to the remaining sides of the quilt.
• Stitch the 2 3/4" x 18" burgundy print strips to opposite sides of the quilt.
• Stitch the 2 3/4" x 22 1/2" burgundy print strips to the remaining sides of the quilt.
• Finish according to *Stitching Tips*, using the 1 3/4" burgundy print strips for the binding.

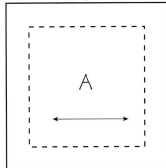

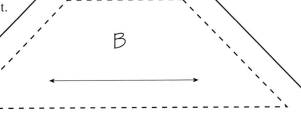

Autumnal Blaze

Stitch the splendor of fall!

I used two gold prints for the leaves in **"Autumnal Blaze"** (16 3/4" x 13 1/2"). The easy bias squares were cut from pieced panels using the simple technique described below. Choose your favorite autumn leaf colors and celebrate the beauty of the season with your own "Autumnal Blaze."

QUILT SIZE: 13 1/2" x 16 3/4"
BLOCK SIZE: 3" square

MATERIALS
Yardage is estimated for 44" fabric.
• Fat quarter (18" x 22") first gold print
• Fat quarter second gold print
• 3/4 yard green print
• 1/4 yard rust print
• 15 1/2" x 18 3/4" piece of backing fabric
• 15 1/2" x 18 3/4" piece of thin batting

CUTTING
Dimensions include a 1/4" seam allowance.
• Cut 21: 1 1/2" squares, first gold print
• Cut 3: 1 3/4" x 14" bias strips, first gold print
• Cut 15: 1 1/2" squares, second gold print
• Cut 2: 1 3/4" x 14" bias strips, second gold print
• Cut 24: 1 1/2" squares, green print
• Cut 5: 1 3/4" x 14" bias strips, green print
• Cut 2: 2" x 15" strips, green print, for the border
• Cut 2: 2" x 19" strips, green print, for the border
• Cut 8: 3/4" x 3 1/2" strips, rust print, for the sashing
• Cut 5: 3/4" x 10" strips, rust print, for the sashing
• Cut 2: 3/4" x 13 3/4" strips, rust print, for the sashing

☞

• Cut 2: 1 3/4" x 44" strips, rust print, for the binding

DIRECTIONS

• Lay a 1 3/4" x 14" first gold print bias strip on a 1 3/4" x 14" green print bias strip, right sides together, 1 1/2" from the end of the green print bias strip. Stitch them together to make a pieced strip, as shown. Make 3.

• Join the pieced strips, alternating colors and offsetting each by 1 1/2", to make a pieced panel, as shown. Press the seam allowances toward the green print.

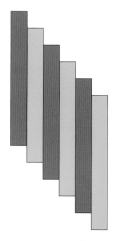

• Place the 45° angle line of your ruler on one seamline in the pieced panel and trim off the uneven edge.

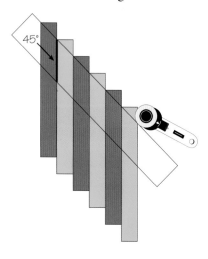

• Cut six 1 1/2" strips from the pieced panel, as shown.

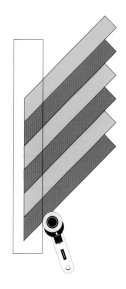

• Lay a ruler on one strip at the first intersection, as shown. Cut to square the end of the strip.

• Measure and cut a 1 1/2" pieced square, as shown.

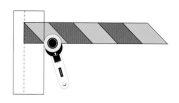

• Place the ruler on the first intersection, as before. Cut to square the end of the strip.
• Measure and cut a 1 1/2" pieced square.
• Continue in the same manner, cutting 5 pieced squares from each strip for a total of 30. You will use 28.
• Using the 1 3/4" x 14" second gold print bias strips and the remaining 1 3/4" x 14" green print bias strips, make a pieced panel, alternating colors and offsetting the ends, as before. Press the seam allowances toward the green print.
• Cut seven 1 1/2" strips from this pieced panel.
• Cut three 1 1/2" pieced squares from each strip, as before, for a total of 21. You will use 20.

• Lay out three 1 1/2" first gold print squares, four matching 1 1/2" pieced squares and two 1 1/2" green print squares, as shown.

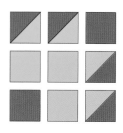

• Stitch the squares into rows and join the rows to complete a block. Make 7.
• Lay out three 1 1/2" second gold print squares, four matching 1 1/2" pieced squares and two 1 1/2" green print squares.
• Stitch the squares into rows and join the rows to complete a block. Make 5.
• Lay out the 12 Leaf blocks, the 3/4" x 3 1/2" rust print strips, the 3/4" x 10" rust print strips and the 3/4" x 13 3/4" rust print strips, as shown in the Assembly Diagram.

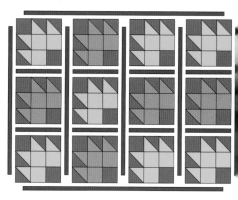

• Stitch the Leaf blocks and the 3/4" x 3 1/2" sashing strips into vertical rows. Join the vertical rows and 3/4" x 10" rust print strips.
• Stitch the 3/4" x 13 3/4" rust print strips to the long sides of the quilt.
• Center and stitch the 2" x 15" green print strips to the short sides of the quilt. Start and stop stitching 1/4" from the edges, backstitching at each end.
• In the same manner, center and stitch the 2" x 19" green print strips to the remaining sides of the quilt.
• Miter each corner, referring to *Stitching Tips*.
• Finish according to *Stitching Tips*, using the 1 3/4" rust print strips for the binding. —————— BIG Easy

Blockheads

Use an easy strip-piecing method for this cute quilt.

A parade of little people march across this quilt! I strip-pieced my **"Blockheads"** (27 1/4" square) to make the project quick, easy and fun. You'll make 12 blocks using this method. Use 9 in the quilt and save 3 for another fun project.

QUILT SIZE: 27 1/4" square
BLOCK SIZE: 5 1/4" square

MATERIALS
Yardage is estimated for 44" fabric.
- Fat eighth (11" x 18") of four dark prints for the blockheads (I used bright green, red, medium blue and dark blue.)
- Fat eighth blue print, for the corner-stones
- Fat quarter (18" x 22") yellow print, for the sashing
- 3/4 yard light print
- 1/2 yard red print, for the border
- 29 1/2" square of backing fabric
- 29 1/2" square of thin batting

CUTTING
Dimensions include a 1/4" seam allowance.
From each dark print fabric:
- Cut 1: 1 3/4" x 5 1/2" strip (head)
- Cut 1: 1" x 4" strip (neck)
- Cut 2: 1 1/8" x 8" strips (legs)
- Cut 3: 2" x 2 1/4" rectangle (body)
- Cut 3: 1 1/8" x 5 3/4" strips (arms)
From the light print fabric:
- Cut 8: 2 1/2" x 5 1/2" strips (head)
- Cut 8: 2 7/8" x 4" strips (neck)
- Cut 4: 1" x 8" strips (legs)
- Cut 24: 2 1/4" x 3 3/4" strips (body)

Also:
- Cut 24: 1 1/2" x 5 3/4" strips, yellow print
- Cut 16: 1 1/2" squares, blue print
- Cut 2: 4" x 20 1/4" strips, red print, for the border
- Cut 2: 4" x 27 1/4" strips, red print, for the border
- Cut 3: 1 3/4" x 44" strips, red print, for the binding

DIRECTIONS
NOTE: *You will make a dozen Blockheads using these instructions. You will use 9 in your quilt.*

For the head sections:
- Stitch a 1 3/4" x 5 1/2" dark print strip between two 2 1/2" x 5 1/2" light print strips to make a pieced panel. Make 4. Cut three 1 1/2" slices from each pieced panel to make 12 head sections. Label them and set them aside.

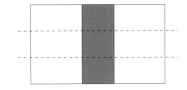

For the neck sections:
- Stitch a 1" x 4" dark print strip between two 2 7/8" x 4" light print strips

to make a pieced panel. Make 4. Cut three 7/8" slices from each pieced panel to make 12 neck sections. Label them and set them aside.

For the leg sections:
- Stitch a 1" x 8" light print strip between two 1 1/8" x 8" same dark print strips. Make 4. Cut three 2 1/4" slices from each pieced panel to make 12 leg sections. Label them and set them aside.

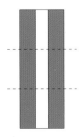

For the lower body sections:
- Stitch a leg section to a matching 2" x 2 1/4" dark print strip to make a lower body section. Make 12.

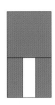

- Stitch a lower body section between two 2 1/4" x 3 3/4" light print strips to make a lower body unit. Make 12.

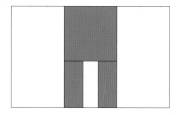

To complete the blocks:
- Lay out the pieces for one block, using matching dark prints, in this order: head section, neck section, 1 1/8" x 5 3/4" arm strip, and lower body unit.
- Join them to complete a Blockhead block. Make 12.

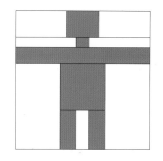

- Stitch together four 1 1/2" blue print squares and three 1 1/2" x 5 3/4" yellow print strips to make a pieced sashing strip, as shown. Make 4.

ASSEMBLY
- Choose 9 of the Blockhead blocks for your quilt. Lay them out in 3 rows of 3. Place 1 1/2" x 5 3/4" yellow print strips vertically between the blocks and at the ends of each row. Place the pieced sashing strips between the rows and at the top and bottom.
- Stitch the strips and blocks into rows. Join the rows and the pieced sashing strips.
- Stitch the 4" x 20 1/4" red print strips to opposite sides of the quilt.
- Stitch the 4" x 27 1/4" red print strips to the remaining sides of the quilt.
- Finish according to *Stitching Tips*, using the 1 3/4" red print strips for the binding. ——————— BIG'Easy

Baskets

A tisket, a tasket,
a dozen pieced baskets!

"Baskets" (27 1/8" x 32 3/4") was a perfect setting for Debra Feece to display some of her favorite scraps. Angela Marie Bosa of Chautauqua, New York, stitched "Chautauqua Baskets" which was the inspiration for Debra's miniature.

QUILT SIZE: 26 3/4" x 32 3/8"
BLOCK SIZE: 4" square

MATERIALS
Yardage is estimated for 44" fabric.
- 12 prints each at least 4" x 6"
- 1/3 yard brown print
- 1/8 yard red
- 1/4 yard gold print
- 1/3 yard tan print
- 2/3 yard purple print

CUTTING
The pattern piece is full size and includes a 1/4" seam allowance, as do all dimensions given.

NOTE: *Group the pieces for each block as you cut them.*
For each of 12 Basket blocks:
- Cut 1: A, print
- Cut 1: 2 5/8" square, same print
- Cut 1: 1 7/8" square, same print; then cut it in half diagonally to yield 2 small triangles

14

Also:

- Cut 24: A, tan print; or cut twelve 2 7/8" squares, then cut each in half diagonally
- Cut 12: 2 5/8" squares, tan print
- Cut 12: 1 1/2" squares, tan print
- Cut 24: 1 1/2" x 2 1/2" strips, tan print
- Cut 6: 4 1/2" squares, brown print
- Cut 2: 3 3/4" squares, brown print, then cut each in half diagonally to yield 4 corner triangles
- Cut 3: 7" squares, brown print, then cut each in quarters diagonally to yield 12 setting triangles. You will use 10.
- Cut 2: 5/8" x 23" strips, red, for the inner border
- Cut 2: 5/8" x 18 1/8" strips, red, for the inner border
- Cut 2: 1 1/4" x 23 3/4" strips, gold print, for the middle border
- Cut 2: 1 1/4" x 19 5/8" strips, gold print, for the middle border
- Cut 2: 4 1/4" x 25 1/4" strips, purple print, for the outer border
- Cut 2: 4 1/4" x 27 1/8" strips, purple print, for the outer border
- Cut 4: 1 3/4" x 35" strips, purple print, for the binding

DIRECTIONS

For each Basket block:

- Stitch a tan print A to a print A to make a large pieced square. Set it aside.

- Lay a 2 5/8" tan print square on a 2 5/8" print square. Stitch 1/4" from the edge on all four sides.

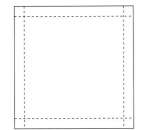

- Cut the square in quarters diagonally to yield 4 small pieced squares. Press the seam allowances toward the darker print.

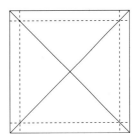

- Stitch 2 small pieced squares together to form a pieced unit, as shown. NOTE: *The edges of the pieced squares are on the bias. Handle them carefully to avoid stretching. They will be stabilized by the adjoining straight edge pieces.*

- Stitch a 1 1/2" tan print square to the pieced unit, as shown.

- Stitch the 2 remaining small pieced squares together to form a second pieced unit, as shown.
- Stitch a small print triangle to a 1 1/2" x 2 1/2" tan print strip. Make a second unit, reversing the placement of the small print triangle, as shown.

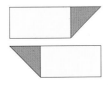

- Assemble the units as shown, to make a basket unit.

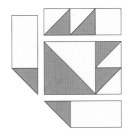

- Stitch a tan print A to the bottom of the basket unit, to complete a Basket block. Make 12.

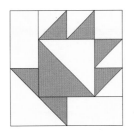

- Lay out the Basket blocks, the 4 1/2" brown print squares, and the brown print setting and corner triangles. Stitch them into diagonal rows and join the rows, as shown in the Assembly Diagram.

- Stitch the 5/8" x 23 1/8" red strips to the long sides of the quilt.
- Stitch the 5/8" x 17 3/4" red strips to the top and bottom of the quilt.
- Stitch the 1 1/4" x 23 3/8" gold print strips to the long sides of the quilt.
- Stitch the 1 1/4" x 19 1/4" gold print strips to the top and bottom of the quilt.
- Stitch the 4 1/4" x 24 7/8" purple print strips to the long sides of the quilt.
- Stitch the 4 1/4" x 26 3/4" purple print strips to the top and bottom of the quilt.
- Finish according to *Stitching Tips*, using the 1 3/4" purple print strips for the binding. BIG·Easy

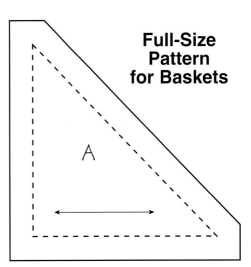

Full-Size Pattern for Baskets

A

Clockwise: On the wall at left, **"Sleepy Little Village"** by Debra Feece; **"Autumnal Blaze," "Pinwheel," "Square in a Square,"** and **"4-Rail Fence,"** all by Christiane Meunier.

16

Clockwise: On the wall, **"Liberty Star"** by Sharon Meinz; **"Blues Bayou"** by Carol Lewis; and **"Windmills"** by Christiane Meunier.

17

Country Home

Stitch a cozy sampler to warm some hearts!

Constance C. Leavitt of Wichita, Kansas, designed **"Country Home"** (19 1/4" x 15 1/4"). She also made the clay buttons that she used to embellish her quilt.

QUILT SIZE: 19 1/4" x 15 1/4"

MATERIALS
Yardage is estimated for 44" fabric.
- Assorted scraps of blue, brown, burgundy, cream, gold, green, and pink prints
- 1/4 yard medium brown
- 1/8 yard dark brown
- 1/4 yard gold print
- 1/8 yard green print
- 17 1/2" x 21 1/2" piece of backing fabric
- 17 1/2" x 21 1/2" piece of thin batting
- Fusible web
- Heart, star, wreath and cat buttons
- Gold embroidery floss

CUTTING
Pattern pieces are full size and include a 1/4" seam allowance, as do all dimensions given. Appliqué pieces are full size and do not include a seam allowance.
For the pieced Star block:
- Cut 4: A, cream print
- Cut 4: B, burgundy print
- Cut 1: 1 1/2" x 3 1/2" strip, same burgundy print
For each of 2 Tree blocks:
- Cut 1: C, green print
- Cut 1: D, second green print
- Cut 1: E, third green print
- Cut 1: F, cream print
- Cut 1: FR, same cream print
- Cut 2: 1 1/4" x 2" rectangles, same cream print
- Cut 1: 1 1/4" x 1 1/2" rectangle, brown print

For the House block:
- Cut 1: 2" x 3 3/8" strip, green print, for the door
- Cut 2: 2 5/8" x 3 3/8" strips, gold print, for the house
- Cut 1: 2 5/8" x 6 1/4" strip, burgundy print
- Cut 2: 2 5/8" squares, cream print
- Cut 2: 1 1/4" x 2 7/8" strips, cream print
- Cut 1: 1 1/4" x 1 1/2" rectangle, brown print, for the chimney
- Cut 2: 1" x 6 1/4" strips, brown print, for the house border
- Cut 2: 1 1/8" x 7 1/4" strips, brown print, for the house border NOTE: *The quilter pieced one of her house border strips with a green print. You may wish to do the same.*
For the pieced border:
- Cut 10: G, assorted dark prints
- Cut 20: H, 2 each of 10 light or medium prints
Also:
- Cut 1: 3 1/2" x 4 1/2" strip, light brown print
- Cut 1: 1 1/2" x 15 1/2" strip, medium brown print
- Cut 1: 2" x 15 1/2" strip, medium brown print
- Cut 1: 2 1/2" x 15 1/4" strip, medium brown print
- Cut 1: 1 3/4" x 28" strip, medium brown print, for the binding
- Cut 1: 1 1/2" x 15 1/2" strip, burgundy print
- Cut 1: 2" x 15 1/2" strip, dark brown print

- Cut 1: 2 1/2" x 15 1/4" strip, gold print
- Cut 1: 1 3/4" x 28" strip, gold print, for the binding
- Cut 1: 1 3/4" x 28" strip, green print, for the binding

PREPARATION
- Trace 7 small and 2 large hearts on the paper side of the fusible web and cut them out just outside of the drawn line.
- Trace one large and 2 small stars on the paper side of the fusible web and cut them out just outside of the drawn line.
- Following manufacturer's instructions, fuse the pattern pieces on the wrong side of appropriate fabric scraps.
- Cut out the pieces on the drawn line.
- Remove the paper backing from the hearts and stars.
- Press all the small hearts on the 2 1/2" x 15 1/4" gold print strip referring to the photo for placement.
- Press a large heart on each 2 5/8" x 3 3/8" gold print strip referring to the photo for placement.
- Press the stars on the 3 1/2" x 4 1/2" brown print strip, referring to the photo for placement.
- With 2 strands of gold floss, embroider around the hearts and stars with a buttonhole stitch.

DIRECTIONS
For the pieced Star block:
- Stitch a tan print A to a burgundy print B to make a pieced square. Make 4.

- Stitch 4 pieced squares together to make a Star block.

- Stitch the 1 1/2" x 3 1/2" burgundy print strip to the star block.

For the Tree blocks:
- Stitch a green print C, D and E together to make a tree top. Make 2.

- Stitch a cream print F to the left side of a tree top and a cream print FR to the right side to complete a tree top section. Make 2.

- Stitch a 1 1/4" x 1 1/2" brown print rectangle between the 1 1/4" x 2" cream print rectangles to make a tree trunk section. Make 2.

- Stitch a tree top section and a tree trunk section together to complete a Tree block. Make 2.

For the House block:
- Stitch the 1 1/4" x 1 1/2" brown print rectangle between the 1 1/4" x 2 7/8" cream print strips to make a chimney section.
- Draw a diagonal line on the wrong sides of the 2 5/8" cream print squares.
- Lay them on the 2 5/8" x 6 1/4" burgundy print strip, right sides together, and stitch on the drawn lines, as shown.

- Trim the seam allowance to 1/4" and press towards the burgundy fabric to make the roof section.
- Stitch the 2" x 3 3/8" green print strip between the 2 5/8" x 3 3/8" gold print strips to make a house section.

- Stitch the chimney section, the roof section and the house section together to assemble the House.

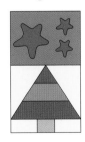

- Stitch the 1" x 6 1/4" brown print strips to the top and bottom of the House.
- Stitch the 1 1/8" x 7 1/4" brown print strips to the sides to complete the House block.

For the pieced border:
- Stitch a print G between matching print H's to make a pieced rectangle. Make 10.

- Stitch 5 pieced rectangles together to make a pieced border strip, as shown. Make 2. NOTE: *Handle the pieced border strip carefully to avoid stretching the bias edge. These borders will be stabilized by the straight grain border strips.*

- Stitch the 3 1/2" x 4 1/2" light brown print strip to the top of a tree block.

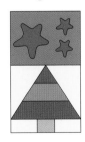

- Stitch the Star block to the top of the remaining tree block.

- Stitch these to opposite sides of the House block to make a House row.

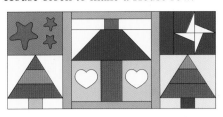

- Lay out the House row, the 1 1/2" x 15 1/2" medium brown print and burgundy print strips and the pieced border strips, as shown.

- Join the rows and strips.
- Stitch the 2" x 15 1/2" medium brown print and dark brown print strips to the top and bottom of the quilt.
- Stitch the 2 1/2" x 15 1/4" medium brown print and gold print strips to the sides of the quilt, as shown in the Assembly Diagram.

- Stitch the 1 3/4" x 28" gold, medium brown print and green print strips together, end to end, to make a pieced strip.
- Finish according to *Stitching Tips*, using the 1 3/4"-wide pieced strip for the binding.
- Embellish the quilt top as desired with cat, heart, star and wreath buttons.

Full-Size Patterns for Country Home are on page 20

Full-Size Patterns for Country Home

(Pattern on page 18)

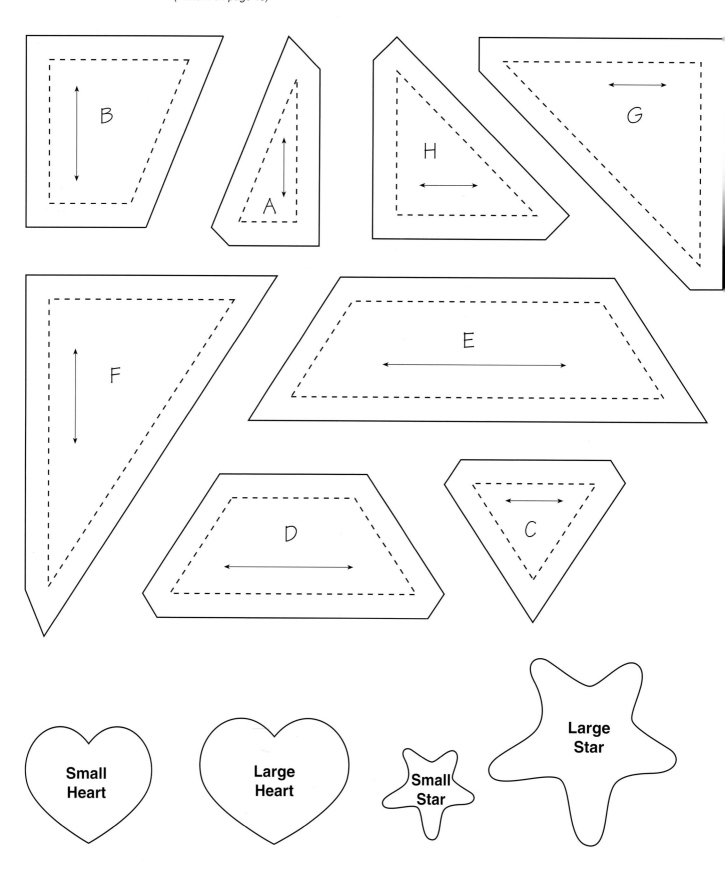

Windmills

It's a breeze to piece a mini with lots of movement!

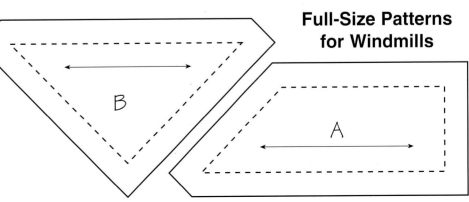

I stitched this patriotic mini and gave it a country look with a plaid border. Your scrap bag will provide some fun as you search for a variety of fabrics to use in **"Windmills"** (20 1/4" square).

QUILT SIZE: 20 1/4" square
BLOCK SIZE: 3 3/4" square

MATERIALS

Yardage is estimated for 44" fabric.
- Assorted scraps of red and blue prints each at least 2" x 4 1/2"
- Assorted scraps of light blue and white prints each at least 3 3/4"
- Fat eighth (11" x 18") tan print
- 1/3 yard blue plaid
- 22 1/4" square of backing fabric
- 22 1/4" square of thin batting

CUTTING

Pattern pieces are full size and include a 1/4" seam allowance, as do all dimensions given.
- Cut 18: A, red prints
- Cut 8: 1 1/8" squares, red prints
- Cut 18: A, blue prints
- Cut 8: 1 1/8" squares, blue prints
- Cut 36: B, light blue or white prints; or cut nine 3 3/4" squares, then cut each in quarters diagonally to yield 36 triangles
- Cut 24: 1 1/8" x 4 1/4" strips, tan print
- Cut 2: 3 1/2" x 14 1/4" strips, blue plaid, for the border
- Cut 2: 3 1/2" x 20 1/4" strips, blue plaid, for the border
- Cut 2: 1 3/4" x 44" strips, blue plaid, for the binding

DIRECTIONS

- Stitch a light blue or white print B to a red print A to make a pieced triangle, as shown. Make 36, using the remaining A's and B's and mixing the prints randomly.
- Stitch a red pieced triangle to a blue pieced triangle to make a half-block, as shown. Make 18.

- Stitch 2 half-blocks together to make a Windmill block, as shown. Make 9.

- Lay out two 1 1/8" red print squares, two 1 1/8" blue print squares and three 1 1/8" x 4 1/4" tan print strips. Join them to make a pieced sashing strip, as shown. Make 4.

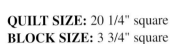

- Lay out the Windmill blocks, 1 1/8" x 4 1/4" tan print sashing strips and the pieced sashing strips, referring to the photo as needed.
- Stitch the tan sashing strips and the Windmill blocks into horizontal rows.
- Join the pieced sashing strips and pieced rows.
- Stitch the 3 1/2" x 14 1/4" blue plaid strips to opposite sides of the quilt.
- Stitch the 3 1/2" x 20 1/4" blue plaid strips to the remaining sides of the quilt.
- Finish according to *Stitching Tips*, using the 1 3/4" blue plaid strips for the binding. ——— BIG*Easy*

Full-Size Patterns for Windmills

B

A

Pinwheel

It is easier than it looks!

A strip-pieced border frames the lively blocks in **"Pinwheel"** (17" square). Although the border has an intricate look, you'll find it surprisingly simple to piece.

QUILT SIZE: 17" square
BLOCK SIZE: 3" square

MATERIALS
Yardage is estimated for 44" fabric.
• Assorted burgundy prints each at least 2 1/2" x 5"
• Assorted light prints each at least 5" square
• Assorted gold prints each at least 6" square
• Fat eighth (11" x 18") light print, for the border
• 1/4 yard second light print, for the border
• 1/4 yard burgundy print, for the border and binding
• 19" square of thin batting
• 19" square of backing fabric

CUTTING
Dimensions include a 1/4" seam allowance. Group the pieces for each block as you cut them.
For each of 9 blocks:
• Cut 2: 2 1/8" squares, one burgundy print
• Cut 2: 2 1/8" squares, one light print
• Cut 2: 2 3/8" squares, same light print; then cut each in half diagonally to yield 4 triangles
For the border:
• Cut 4: 1 3/8" x 15" strips, light print
• Cut 4: 1 3/8" x 15" strips, second light print

• Cut 10: 1 3/8" x 2 3/4" rectangles, second light print
• Cut 4: 2 3/8" x 15" strips, burgundy print
• Cut 6: 1 3/8" x 2 1/4" rectangles, burgundy print
Also:
• Cut 4: 3 1/2" squares, gold prints
• Cut 2: 3" squares, gold prints, then cut each in half diagonally for the corner triangles
• Cut 2: 5 1/2" squares, gold prints, then cut each in quarters diagonally for the setting triangles
• Cut 2: 1 3/4" x 44" strips, burgundy print, for the binding

DIRECTIONS
For each of 9 blocks:
• Draw a diagonal line from corner to corner on the wrong side of a 2 1/8" light print square. Lay the light print square on a 2 1/8" burgundy square, right sides together and sew 1/4" away from the line on both sides. Make 2.

• Cut each square on the drawn line. You will have 4 pieced squares.
• Stitch the pieced squares together to make a Pinwheel.
NOTE: *To add interest to the design, you*

may wish to reverse the direction of some of your Pinwheels.

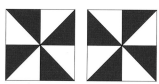

• Trim the Pinwheel blocks to 2 5/8" square.
• Stitch 2 light print triangles to opposite sides of the Pinwheel.

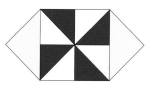

• Stitch 2 matching light print triangles to the remaining sides of the Pinwheel to complete a block.

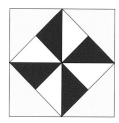

ASSEMBLY
• Lay out the Pinwheel blocks, the 3 1/2" gold print squares, the gold print setting triangles and the gold print corner triangles in diagonal rows, as shown

22

in the Assembly Diagram.

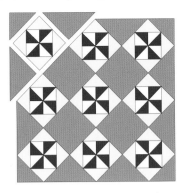

• Stitch them into rows. Join the rows.

For the border:

• Stitch a 2 3/8" x 15" burgundy print strip between a 1 3/8" x 15" light print strip and a 1 3/8" x 15" second light print strip to make a pieced strip, as shown. Make 4. Press the seam allowances toward the light prints. Cut ten 1 3/8" slices from each pieced strip, as shown.

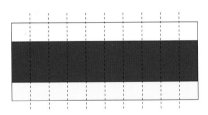

• Place two slices, right sides together, as shown. Line up the upper end of the piece on top with the raw edge of the seam allowance of the piece on the bottom. Join the strips.

• Add 8 additional strips, offsetting each one in the same manner to make a pieced border. Make 2.

• Trim the long edge of the light fabric 1/4" beyond the points of the burgundy fabric, as shown. Trim the second pieced border in the same manner. Label these Border A.

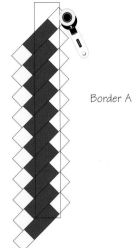

Border A

• Place two slices, right sides together, as shown. Line up the lower end of the piece on top with the raw edge of the seam allowance of the piece on the bottom. Join the strips.

• Add 8 additional strips, offsetting each one in the same manner to make a pieced border. Make 2. Trim the inside edge as before. Label these Border B.

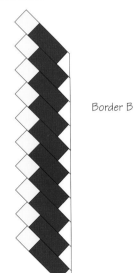

Border B

• Stitch a 1 3/8" x 2 3/4" second light print rectangle to a 1 3/8" x 2 1/4" burgundy print rectangle to make a pieced rectangle. Make 4.

• Stitch two pieced rectangles, across their short ends, to make a long pieced strip, keeping the burgundy prints together. Make 2.

• Stitch a 1 3/8" x 2 1/4" burgundy print rectangle between two 1 3/8" x 2 3/4" second light print rectangles, to make a short pieced strip. Make 2.

• Lay out a long pieced strip, a short pieced strip and a 1 3/8" x 2 3/4" second light print rectangle.

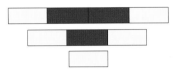

• Join the strips, matching the centers to make a pieced corner unit. Make 2.
• Center and stitch the Border A's to opposite sides of the quilt. Start and stop stitching 1/4" from the edges, backstitching at each end.
• Center and stitch the Border B's to the remaining sides of the quilt. Start and stop stitching 1/4" from the edges, backstitching at each end.
• Miter the borders at the two opposite corners.
• Center and stitch a corner unit to each remaining corner of the quilt. Square the quilt, trimming the borders 1/4" beyond the points of the burgundy fabric, as before.
• Finish according to *Stitching Tips*, using the 1 3/4" burgundy strips for the binding. ——————— BIG Easy

Full-Size Quilting Design for Pinwheel

Christmas Pinwheels

A traditional design with a holiday twist!

I had fun making **"Christmas Pinwheels"** (12 1/2" square). Two shades of red lend subtle depth to this traditional design, while the green framing strips add a three-dimensional touch.

QUILT SIZE: 12 1/2" square
BLOCK SIZE: 4" square

MATERIALS
- Fat eighth (11" x 18") white print
- Fat eighth dark red print
- Fat eighth bright red print
- 1/4 yard green print
- 14 1/2" square of backing fabric
- 14 1/2" square of thin batting

CUTTING
All dimensions include a 1/4" seam allowance.
- Cut 4: 3 1/4" squares, white print, then cut each in quarters diagonally to yield 16 triangles. Label them A and set them aside.
- Cut 4: 3 1/4" squares, dark red print, then cut each in quarters diagonally to yield 16 triangles. Label them A and set them aside.
- Cut 4: 4 1/4" squares, dark red print, then cut each in quarters diagonally to yield 16 triangles for the outer border. Label them C and set them aside.
- Cut 2: 1" x 8 1/2" strips, dark red print, for the inner border
- Cut 2: 1" x 9 1/2" strips, dark red print, for the inner border
- Cut 8: 2 7/8" squares, bright red print, then cut each in half diagonally to yield 16 triangles. Label them B and set them aside.
- Cut 3: 4 1/4" squares, bright red print, then cut each in quarters diagonally to yield 12 triangles for the outer border. Label them C and set them aside.
- Cut 4: 3/4" x 6 1/2" strips, green

print, for the framing strip
- Cut 4: 3/4" x 13 1/2" strips, green print, for the framing strip
- Cut 2: 1 3/4" x 44" strips, green print, for the binding

DIRECTIONS
- Stitch a white print A triangle to a dark red print A triangle to make a pieced triangle. Make 16.

- Stitch a pieced triangle to a bright red print B triangle to make a pieced triangle unit. Make 16.

- Stitch 2 pieced triangle units together to make a half-block. Make 8.

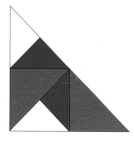

- Press the 3/4" x 6 1/2" green print strips in half lengthwise, wrong sides together, to make framing strips.
- Place a framing strip on one of the half-blocks, right sides together, with raw edges aligned. Baste in place.

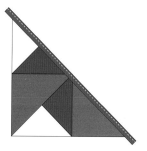

- Stitch another half-block to it to complete a block. Make 4.
- Lay out the blocks in 2 rows of 2 according to the Assembly Diagram. Be sure the framing strip lies toward the quilt center.

- Stitch the blocks into rows. Join the rows.

- Press the 3/4" x 13 1/2" green print strips in half lengthwise, wrong sides together, to make framing strips. Set them aside.
- Stitch 2 dark red print C triangles and 3 bright red print C triangles together to make a border unit. Make 4. Set them aside.

- Stitch 2 dark red print C triangles together to make a corner unit. Make 4.

Set them aside.

- Stitch the 1" x 8 1/2" dark red strips to opposite sides of the quilt.
- Stitch the 1" x 9 1/2" dark red strips to the remaining sides of the quilt.
- Place framing strips on opposite sides of the quilt, right sides together, with the raw edges aligned. Baste in place.

- Place framing strips on the remaining sides of the quilt, right sides together, with the raw edges aligned. Baste in place.
- Center and stitch the border units to each side of the quilt, placing the long side against the quilt.
- Stitch a corner unit to each corner of the quilt.
- Finish according to *Stitching Tips*, using the 1 3/4" green print strips for the binding. ——————— BIG*Easy*

Hunter's Star Variation

Use quick-pieced squares to create stars!

Marilyn Michael of Greenville, Pennsylvania, made **"Hunter's Star Variation"** (25" square). Marilyn stitched her quilt to meet a guild challenge that required the project be made entirely from right triangles. Working on a flannel wall allowed her to stand back and see how the design was progressing. I've simplified the directions by adding quick-pieced squares—no tiny triangles to cut!

QUILT SIZE: 25" square
BLOCK SIZE: 5" square

MATERIALS
Yardage is estimated for 44" fabric.
- Scraps of light beige and light tan prints each at least 4 1/4" square
- Scraps of dark blue, brown, red and green prints each at least 4 1/4" square
- 3" square red print, for the corner-stones
- 1/4 yard green print, for the inner border
- 1/2 yard blue print, for the outer border
- 27" square of backing fabric
- 27" square of thin batting

CUTTING
Dimensions include a 1/4" seam allowance.
- Cut 32: 4 1/4" squares, light prints
- Cut 8: 4 1/4" squares, dark blue prints
- Cut 24: 4 1/4" squares, dark brown, red and green prints
- Cut 4: 1 1/4" squares, red print
- Cut 4: 1 1/4" x 20 1/2" strips, green print, for the inner border
- Cut 4: 2" x 28" strips, blue print, for the outer border
- Cut 3: 1 3/4" x 44" strips, blue print, for the binding

DIRECTIONS
- Draw diagonal lines from corner to

corner on the wrong side of a 4 1/4" light print square. Draw a vertical line and a horizontal line through the center. Make 24.

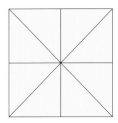

- Mark 8 assorted 4 1/4" dark squares in the same manner. Set them aside.
- Lay a 4 1/4" marked light print square on a 4 1/4" unmarked dark print ☞

square, right sides together. Stitch 1/4" away from the diagonal lines on both sides, as shown. Make 7 using blue 4 1/4" squares, 3 brown, 3 red and 3 green.

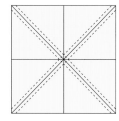

• Cut each sewn square on the drawn diagonal, horizontal and vertical lines. You will have 128 light/dark pieced squares.

NOTE: *Set aside 32 blue light/dark pieced squares, 8 red light/dark pieced squares and 8 brown light/dark pieced squares for the star points.*

• Lay one of the remaining marked light print 4 1/4" squares on a different 4 1/4" unmarked light print square and stitch, as before. Make 8.

• Cut on the drawn lines to yield 64 light pieced squares.

• Stitch 4 light pieced squares together to make a light Four Square, as shown. Make 16 and set them aside.

• Lay a 4 1/4" marked dark print square on a different unmarked dark print square and stitch, as before. Make 8.

• Cut on the drawn lines to yield 64 dark pieced squares.

• Stitch 4 dark pieced squares together to make a dark Four Square, as shown. Make 16 and set them aside.

• Stitch 2 blue light/dark pieced squares together to make a blue star point, as shown. Make 16.

• Join 2 assorted light/dark squares and stitch them to a blue star point, as

shown. Make 16. Label these Group 1 and set them aside.

Group 1

• Stitch 2 blue light/dark pieced squares together to make a blue star point, as shown. Make 8. Set them aside.

• In the same manner, make 4 red and 4 brown star points and set them aside.

• Join 2 pieced squares and stitch them to a blue star point, as shown. Make 8. Label these Group 2 and set them aside.

Group 2

• In the same manner, join 2 pieced squares and stitch them to a red star point. Make 4. Label these Group 3 and set them aside.

• In the same manner, join 2 pieced squares and stitch them to a brown star point. Make 4. Label these Group 4 and set them aside.

• Lay out a light Four Square, a dark Four Square, a Group 1 and a Group 2 Four Square, as shown.

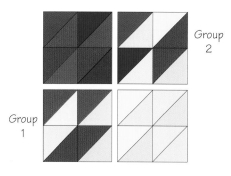

Group 2

Group 1

• Stitch the Four Squares into pairs, then join the pairs to complete a block. Make 8.

• Lay out a light Four Square, a dark Four Square, a Group 1 and a Group 3 Four Square, as shown. Stitch the Four Squares into pairs, then join the pairs to complete a block. Make 4.

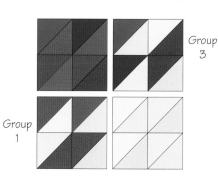

Group 3

Group 1

• Lay out a light Four Square, a dark Four Square, a Group 1 and a Group 4 Four Square, as shown. Stitch the Four Squares into pairs, then join the pairs to complete a block. Make 4.

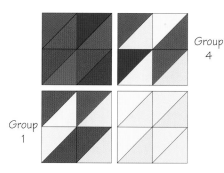

Group 4

Group 1

• Lay out the completed blocks in 4 rows of 4. Alternate the direction of the diagonal seams in every other block. Arrange the blocks so that they form blue, red and brown stars referring to the photo as necessary.

• Stitch the blocks into rows. Join the rows.

• Stitch 1 1/4" x 20 1/2" green print strips to opposite sides of the quilt.

• Stitch a 1 1/4" red print square to each end of a 1 1/4" x 20 1/2" green print strip to make a pieced strip. Make 2.

• Stitch the pieced strips to the remaining sides of the quilt.

• Center and stitch 2" x 28" blue print strips to opposite sides of the quilt. Start and stop stitching 1/4" from the edges.

• Center and stitch 2" x 28" blue print strips to the remaining sides of the quilt. Start and stop stitching 1/4" from the edges.

• Miter the corners according to *Stitching Tips*.

• Finish according to *Stitching Tips*, using the 1 3/4" blue print strips for the binding. ——————— BIG Easy

Basic Blues

Stitch old-fashioned charm in this two-color mini.

I stitched **"Basic Blues"** (14 1/2" x 17 1/2") to showcase a group of blue and white reproduction prints. Try this quick and easy project with your favorite fabrics!

QUILT SIZE: 14 1/2" x 17 1/2"
BLOCK SIZE: 3" square

MATERIALS
Yardage is estimated for 44" fabric.
- Assorted scraps of white prints each at least 2 3/8" square
- 1/4 yard dark blue print
- 1/4 yard medium blue print
- 1/4 yard light blue print
- 1/8 yard second dark blue print, for the binding
- 16 1/2" x 19 1/2" piece of backing fabric
- 16 1/2" x 19 1/2" piece of thin batting

CUTTING
Pattern pieces are full size and include a 1/4" seam allowance, as do all dimensions given. Within each block, the A and C piece are cut from the same blue print and the B's are cut in matching pairs of the same white print. For a scrappier look, randomly mix the prints.
- Cut 9: A, dark blue; or cut 2" squares
- Cut 9: C, dark blue; or cut five 3 7/8" squares, then cut each in half diagonally to yield 10 triangles. You will use 9.
- Cut 2: 1 3/4" x 44" strips, second dark blue print, for the binding
- Cut 6: A, medium blue; or cut 2" squares

- Cut 6: C, medium blue; or cut three 3 7/8" squares, then cut each in half diagonally to yield 6 triangles
- Cut 2: 1 1/2" x 14 1/2" strips, medium blue, for the border
- Cut 5: A, light blue; or cut 2" squares
- Cut 5: C, light blue; or cut three 3 7/8" squares, then cut each in half diagonally to yield 6 triangles. You will use 5.
- Cut 2: 1 1/2" x 15 1/2" strips, light blue, for the border
- Cut 40: B, assorted white prints; or cut twenty 2 3/8" squares, then cut each in half diagonally

DIRECTIONS
- Stitch 2 matching white print B's to adjacent sides of a blue print A, making a pieced triangle, as shown.

- Stitch the pieced triangle to a matching blue print C to complete a block. Make 20.

- Lay out the blocks in 5 rows of 4, as shown in the Assembly Diagram.

- Stitch the blocks into rows. Join the rows.
- Stitch the 1 1/2" x 15 1/2" light blue print strips to the long sides of the quilt.
- Stitch the 1 1/2" x 14 1/2" medium blue print strips to the remaining sides of the quilt.
- Finish according to *Stitching Tips*, using the 1 3/4" second dark blue print strips for the binding. ——— BIG'Easy

**Full-Size Patterns for
Basic Blues are
on page 32**

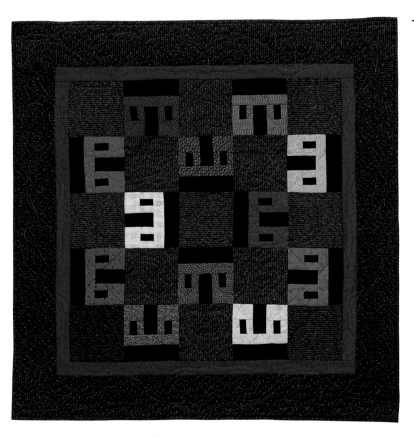

Sleepy Little Village

Rise and shine!

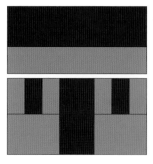

These houses fill the entire block! Debra Feece was inspired to stitch **"Sleepy Little Village"** (32 1/2" square) after seeing Karen Baltazar's "Wee Hours" in Issue 24 of *Miniature Quilts* magazine. Surrounded by blue print fabric, the neighborhood has a peaceful feel.

QUILT SIZE: 32 1/2" square
BLOCK SIZE: 4" square

MATERIALS
Yardage is estimated for 44" fabric.
• 12 scraps of light, medium and dark prints each at least 5" square for the houses
• 1/2 yard of black
• 1/3 yard red print
• 1 yard blue print
• 34 1/2" square piece of backing fabric
• 34 1/2" square of thin batting

CUTTING
All dimensions include a 1/4" seam allowance.
For each of the 12 houses:
• Cut 1: 1 1/4" x 4 1/2" strip, house scrap
• Cut 2: 1 5/8" x 2" rectangles, same house scrap
• Cut 4: 1" x 1 1/2" rectangles, same house scrap
Also:
• Cut 12: 1 5/8" x 4 1/2" strips, black, for the roofs
• Cut 12: 1 1/2" x 2 5/8" rectangles, black, for the doors
• Cut 24: 1" x 1 1/2" rectangles, black, for the windows

• Cut 2: 1 3/4" x 20 1/2" strips, red print, for the inner border
• Cut 2: 1 3/4" x 23" strips, red print, for the inner border
• Cut 13: 4 1/2" squares, blue print
• Cut 2: 5 1/4" x 23" strips, blue print, for the outer border
• Cut 2: 5 1/4" x 32 1/2" strips, blue print, for the outer border
• Cut 4: 1 3/4" x 44" strips, blue print, for the binding

DIRECTIONS
For each of the 12 houses:
• Stitch a 1" x 1 1/2" black rectangle between two 1" x 1 1/2" house scrap rectangles, right sides together along their length, to form a pieced rectangle. Make 2.

• Stitch a 1 5/8" x 2" house scrap rectangle to the bottom of a pieced rectangle to make a window unit. Make 2.

• Stitch a 1 1/2" x 2 5/8" black rectangle between 2 window units to form the lower portion of the house.

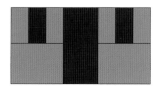

• Stitch a 1 1/4" x 4 1/2" house scrap strip to a 1 5/8" x 4 1/2" black strip, right sides together along their length, to form the roof unit.
• Join the lower portion of the house to the roof unit to complete a House block.

• Lay out the 12 House blocks and the 4 1/2" blue print squares in 5 rows of 5, referring to the photo for placement. ☞

4-Rail Fence

So quick and easy you can make several!

My **"4-Rail Fence"** (20" x 22 1/2") is strip-pieced using a variety of lively prints. This is a super-fast method for making a mini. Just stitch strips into panels and slice them to make the blocks! Some of the blocks have one light strip, while others are all dark giving your eye a place to rest as you view the quilt.

QUILT SIZE: 20" x 22 1/2"
BLOCK SIZE: 2 1/2" square

MATERIALS

Yardage is estimated for 44" fabric.
• Assorted scraps of green, pink, purple, yellow, gray, tan, blue and navy prints each at least 1 1/8" x 15"
• Fat eighth (11" x 18") tan print
• 1/2 yard green print
• 22" x 24 1/2" piece of backing fabric
• 22" x 24 1/2" piece of thin batting

CUTTING

Dimensions include a 1/4" seam allowance.
• Cut 24: 1 1/8" x 15" strips, assorted prints
• Cut 2: 1" x 15 1/2" strips, tan print, for the inner border
• Cut 2: 1" x 14" strips, tan print, for the inner border
• Cut 2: 3 1/2" x 16 1/2" strips, green

print for the outer border
• Cut 2: 3 1/2" x 20" strips, green print for the outer border
• Cut 3: 1 3/4" x 44" strips, green print for the binding

PREPARATION

• Separate the 1 1/8" x 15" strips into 6 groups of 4 strips, making sure there are a variety of colors represented in each group. Make some groups with only dark fabrics while including one light strip in others.

DIRECTIONS

• Stitch two 1 1/8" x 15" strips from one group, right sides together, along their length to make a pieced strip. Make 2.
• Stitch the pieced strips, right sides together, along their length to make a pieced panel.
• Make pieced panels from the remain-

ing groups of strips. Cut five 3" slices from each panel to yield a total of 30 blocks.

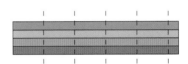

• Lay out the blocks in 6 rows of 5, alternating the direction of the blocks.
• Stitch the blocks into rows. Join the rows.
• Stitch the 1" x 15 1/2" tan print strips to the long sides of the quilt.
• Stitch the 1" x 14" tan print strips to the remaining sides of the quilt.
• Stitch the 3 1/2" x 16 1/2" green print strips to the long sides of the quilt.
• Stitch the 3 1/2" x 20" green print strips to the remaining sides of the quilt.
• Finish according to *Stitching Tips*, using the 1 3/4" green print strips for the binding. ——————— BIG'Easy

---

Sleepy Little Village (continued)

• Stitch the blocks and squares into rows. Join the rows.
• Stitch the 1 3/4" x 20 1/2" red print strips to opposite sides of the quilt.
• Stitch the 1 3/4" x 23" red print

strips to the remaining sides of the quilt.
• Stitch the 5 1/4" x 23" blue print strips to opposite sides of the quilt.
• Stitch the 5 1/4" x 32 1/2" blue print

strips to the remaining sides of the quilt.
• Finish according to *Stitching Tips*, using the 1 3/4" blue print strips for the binding. ——————— BIG'Easy

Deb's Four Patch

Set scrappy
Four Patches on point!

Debra Feece loves the scrappy look in her quilts. **"Deb's Four Patch"** (21 3/4" square) is a perfect miniature to show-off your favorite fabrics.

QUILT SIZE: 21 3/4" square
BLOCK SIZE: 2" square

MATERIALS
Yardage is estimated for 44" fabric.
- Assorted scraps of light, medium and dark prints each at least 1 1/2" square
- Fat quarter (18" x 22") tan print
- 1/8 yard burgundy print
- 1/3 yard dark tan print
- 24" square of backing fabric
- 24" square of thin batting

CUTTING
Dimensions include a 1/4" seam allowance. NOTE: *Select squares that will have good color contrast for each Four Patch block. In this miniature, some of the blocks were pieced with 2 sets of matching squares, while in others each square is a different color. See "Make Them Match" for an easy way to stitch a Four Patch block with 2 sets of matching squares.*
- Cut 144: 1 1/2" squares, print scraps
- Cut 25: 2 1/2" squares, tan print
- Cut 5: 4 1/8" squares, tan print; then cut each in quarters diagonally to yield 20 setting triangles
- Cut 2: 2 3/8" squares, tan print; then cut each in half diagonally to yield 4 corner triangles
- Cut 2: 1" x 17 3/4" strips, burgundy print, for the inner border
- Cut 2: 1" x 18 3/4" strips, burgundy print, for the inner border

- Cut 2: 2" x 18 3/4" strips, dark tan print, for the outer border
- Cut 2: 2" x 21 3/4" strips, dark tan print, for the outer border
- Cut 2: 1 3/4" x 44" strips, dark tan print, for the binding

DIRECTIONS
- Stitch two 1 1/2" print squares together to make a pieced unit. Make 72.

- Stitch two pieced units together to make a Four Patch. Make 36.

- Lay out the 36 Four Patches on point. Add the 2 1/2" squares, the setting triangles and the corner triangles to make diagonal rows, referring to the photo as needed.
- Stitch them into rows. Join the rows.
- Stitch the 1" x 17 3/4" burgundy print strips to opposite sides of the quilt.
- Stitch the 1" x 18 3/4" burgundy print strips to the remaining sides of the quilt.
- Stitch the 2" x 18 3/4" dark tan print strips to opposite sides of the quilt.
- Stitch the 2" x 21 3/4" dark tan print strips to the remaining sides of the quilt.
- Finish according to *Stitching Tips*, using the 1 3/4" dark tan print strips for the binding. ——— BIG Easy

"Make Them Match"

For an easy way to make **"Deb's Four-Patch"** with 2 sets of matching squares per block; follow these cutting and sewing directions:
- Cut seventy-two 1 1/2" x 3 1/4" strips, print scraps
- Stitch two contrasting 1 1/2" x 3 1/4" strips, right sides together, along their length, as shown. Make 36.

- Press the seam allowance toward the darker fabric.
- Cut two 1 1/2" slices from each pieced strip.

- Stitch each pair of matching pieced strips together to make a Four-Patch.

Stitching Tips
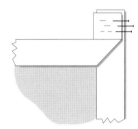

Fabric Selection

100% cotton works well for most projects because it is easy to finger press and handles nicely. The yardage requirements in these patterns are based on a standard 44" wide bolt. However, many of the quilts can be made from assorted scraps.

Fabric Preparation

It's a good idea to wash fabrics before using them in your minis. Test all of your fabrics to be sure they are colorfast.

Templates

Trace pattern pieces on clear plastic. Use a permanent marker to list the name of the block, total number of pieces, pattern letter and grainline on each template. If the instructions call for an R, for example BR, the B template must be flipped to make the reverse of B.

Pieced Patterns

Patterns include 1/4" seam allowances unless otherwise noted. The solid line is the cutting line and the broken line is the sewing line. For machine piecing, make the template with the seam allowance. Trace around the template on the wrong side of the fabric. For hand piecing, make the template without the seam allowance. Trace the template on the wrong side of your fabric and add 1/4" seam allowance as you cut.

Marking Fabric

Silver or white marking tools usually work well for dark fabrics and fine line pencils for light fabrics. Always use a sharp pencil and a light touch. Lay a piece of fine-grained sandpaper under the fabric to keep it from slipping while you mark it.

Hand Sewing

Use a thin, short needle ("sharp") to ensure a flat seam. Sew only on the marked sewing line using small, even stitches.

Machine Sewing

Set the stitch length to 14 stitches per inch. You can make an accurate 1/4" guide for your sewing machine in the following way: Cut a length of moleskin foot pad about 1/4" x 2". Place a clear plastic ruler under and to the left of the needle aligning the right edge of the ruler 1/4" from the point of the needle along the throat plate. Stick the moleskin in place at the ruler's edge. Feed fabric under the needle, touching this guide.

When directions call for you to start or stop stitching 1/4" from edges, as for set-in pieces, backstitch to secure the seam.

Pressing

Press seams toward the darker of the two fabrics. Press abutting seams in opposite directions whenever possible. Use a dry iron and press carefully, as little blocks are easy to distort.

Mitering Corners

Center each border strip on a side so the ends extend equally. Sew, leaving 1/4" unstitched at the beginning and end of the stitching line. Remember to backstitch at each end to secure the seam. Do not stitch into the seam allowance.

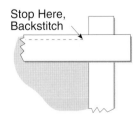

Stop Here, Backstitch

On the ironing board, smooth the border strips out for one corner and lay one extension over the other. Fold the top extension under at a 45° angle so the end is aligned with the strip below. Press a crease to mark the angle. Pin the ends together in several places.

Fold the quilt on the diagonal, right sides together, and sew on the crease, starting at the seamline and running off the outer edge. Open the corner and check to see that it lies flat before trimming away excess fabric. Repeat for the remaining corners.

FINISHING

Marking

Cut simple designs from clear plastic adhesive-backed shelf paper. They'll stick and re-stick long enough to finish the quilt. Use masking tape to mark grids. Remove the tape when you're not quilting to avoid leaving a sticky residue. Mark lightly with pencils; thick lines that won't go away really stand out on a small quilt.

Batting

Use a low-loft or very thin batting. Some quilters peel batting into two layers (leaving some loft and good drape); others use flannel as a filler. Layer the quilt sandwich as follows: backing, wrong side up; batting; quilt top, right side up. Baste or pin the layers together.

Quilting

Very small quilts can be lap-quilted without a hoop. Larger ones can be quilted in a hoop or small frame. Use a short, thin needle ("between") and small stitches that will be in scale with the little quilt. Thread the needle with a single strand of quilting thread and ☞

knot one end. Insert the needle through the quilt top and batting (not the backing) an inch away from where you want to begin quilting. Gently pull the thread to pop the knot through the top and bury it in the batting. Too much quilting can flatten a miniature and set the quilt "out of square." Too little quilting causes puffiness which can detract from the scale of the quilt. Experiment and decide what you like best. When the quilting is finished, trim the back and batting even with the top.

Binding

For most straight-edged quilts, a double-fold French binding is an attractive, durable and easy finish. To make 1/4" finished binding, cut each strip 1 3/4" wide. Sew binding strips together with diagonal seams; trim and press seams open.

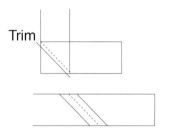

Fold the binding strip in half lengthwise, wrong sides together and press. Position the binding strip on the right side of the quilt top, aligning the raw edges of the binding with the edge of the quilt top. Leave approximately 4" of the binding strip free. Beginning several inches from one corner, stitch the binding to the quilt with a 1/4" seam allowance. When you reach a corner, stop the stitching line exactly 1/4" from the edge. Backstitch, clip threads and remove the quilt from the machine. Fold the binding up and away, creating a 45° angle, as shown.

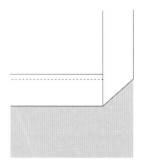

Fold the binding down as shown, and begin stitching at the edge.

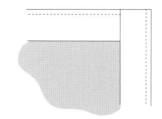

Continue stitching around the quilt to within 4" of the starting point. To finish, fold both strips back along the edge of the quilt so that the folded edges meet an equal distance from both lines of stitching and the binding lies flat on the quilt. Finger press to crease the folds. Cut both strips 7/8" from the folds.

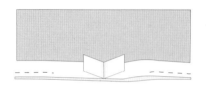

Open both strips and place the ends at right angles to each other, right sides together. Fold the bulk of the quilt out of your way. Join the strips with a diagonal seam, as shown.

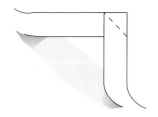

Trim the seam allowance to 1/4" and press it open. Fold the joined strips so that the wrong sides are together again. Place the binding flat against the quilt and finish stitching it to the quilt. Clip the corners. Trim the batting and backing even with the edge of the quilt top so that the binding edge will be filled with batting when you fold the binding to the back of the quilt. Blindstitch the binding to the back of the quilt, covering the seamline.

Sign Your Quilt

Small quilts are revered by collectors, and the little quilts we make today will be treasured by our families and friends. Using embroidery, cross-stitch or permanent marker, write your name and other important data (like your city, the date the quilt was completed and for whom the quilt was made) on a label and attach it to the back of your quilt. Someone will be glad you did!

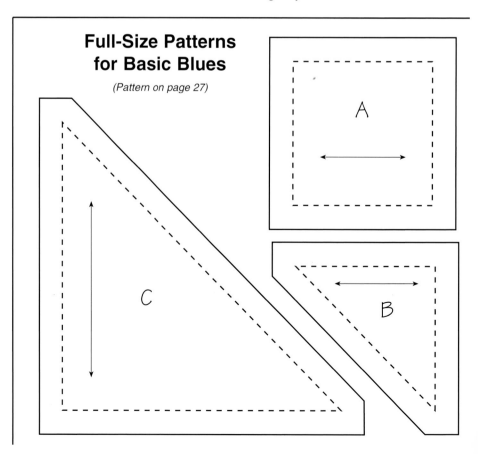

Full-Size Patterns for Basic Blues

(Pattern on page 27)